A ROOKIE READER®

BUGS!

By Patricia and Fredrick McKissack

Illustrated by Clovis Martin

Prepared under the direction of Robert Hillerich, Ph.D.

CHILDRENS PRESS®
CHICAGO

LIBRARY OF CONGRESS
Library of Congress Cataloging-in-Publication Data

McKissack, Pat, 1944-
    Bugs! / by Patricia & Fredrick McKissack ;
illustrated by Clovis Martin.
        p.   cm. — (A rookie reader)
    Summary: Simple text and illustrations of a variety
of insects introduce the numbers one through five.
    ISBN 0-516-02088-9
    [1. Insects—Fiction. 2. Counting.] I. McKissack,
Fredrick. II. Martin, Clovis, ill. III. Title. IV. Series.
PZ7.M478693Bu   1988
[E]—dc19   88-22875
                                                            CIP
                                                            AC

Childrens Press®, Chicago
Copyright © 1988 by Regensteiner Publishing Enterprises, Inc.
All rights reserved. Published simultaneously in Canada.
Printed in the United States of America.
    4 5 6 7 8 9 10 R 97 96 95 94 93

Bugs.

Where?

Up here.

One fat red bug.

Bugs. Bugs.

Where?

Under here.

Two long, skinny, yellow bugs.

Bugs. Bugs. Bugs.

Where?

Over there.

Three fat, green bugs with two big eyes.

Bugs. Bugs. Bugs. Bugs.

Where?

In here.

Four bugs with four hundred feet.

Bugs. Bugs. Bugs. Bugs. Bugs.

Where?

Out there.

Five little bugs that fly here and there.

Bugs. Bugs.

Lots of bugs.

Where?
Where?

Everywhere!

WORD LIST

and	green	red
big	here	skinny
bug	hundred	that
bugs	in	there
everywhere	little	three
eyes	long	two
fat	lots	under
feet	of	up
five	one	where
fly	out	with
four	over	yellow

About the Author

Patricia and Fredrick McKissack are freelance writers, editors, and teachers of writing. They are the owners of All-Writing Services, located in Clayton, Missouri. Since 1975, the McKissacks have published numerous magazine articles and stories for juvenile and adult readers. They also have conducted educational and editorial workshops throughout the country. The McKissacks and their three teenage sons live in a large remodeled inner-city home in St. Louis.

About the Artist

Clovis Martin, a graduate of the Cleveland Institute of Art, currently resides with his wife and two children in Cleveland Heights, Ohio. BUGS!, his sixth book for Childrens Press, brought back childhood memories of days spent discovering these fascinating, multi-legged creatures.